Imagining a Unicorn

Imagining a Unicorn

BARRY SPACKS

Athens
The University of Georgia Press

Acknowledgments

The author and the publisher gratefully acknowledge permission to
reprint the following poems which originally appeared in the publica-
tions here noted:
"Like This" originally appeared in *Harper's Magazine.*
The poem "Like a Prism," © 1974, The New Yorker Magazine, Inc.
"The Pale Ones," *Atlantic Monthly;* "Glee," *Bartleby's Review;* "The
Parent Birds," *B.U. Journal;* "The Beautiful Suicide," *Boston Review of
the Arts;* "Elegy," *California Quarterly;* "Old Men at the Edge of the
Highway" and "The Two of Them," *Carleton Miscellany;* "A Normal
Noon" and "Old-Time Stereopticon," *Centennial Review;* "Across the
Hall," *College English;* "The Man With Orange Wands," *Counter/
Measures;* "Finding a Yiddish Paper on the Riverside Line," *Crazy
Horse;* "Spacks Street," *Georgia Review;* "Woman in the Subway," *Hud-
son Review;* "People," *Kayak;* "The Ventnor Waterworks," *Mas-
sachusetts Review;* "Don Potts and His Visionary Cars" and "Home-
truths," *Michigan Quarterly Review;* "Ill Will," *Midwest Quarterly;*
"Working Title," *Nation;* "We Others" and "Rehearsal," *New Republic;*
"Gerard," *Place;* "The Times" and "Counting the Losses," *Plough-
shares;* "Local Messages," "Malediction," and "Imagining a Unicorn,"
Poetry; "Seeing Pablo Neruda," *Salmagundi;* "Gliding," *Sewanee Re-
view;* "New Copley in the Gallery," *Shenandoah;* "Two Memory
Poems," *Syracuse Guide;* "After an Ancient Text," *Texas Quarterly;*
"The Need to Praise" and "Complain," *Zeugma.*

Library of Congress Cataloging in Publication Data

Spacks, Barry.
    Imagining a unicorn.
    I. Title.
PS3569.P33I4   811'.5'4   78-736
ISBN 0-8203-0444-1

For my students

Contents

I

Wolf of the World

All the tale is bare your breast,
Bare your heart, the fever's brief;
Simply everyday, the rest:
Wolf of the world, and the fear of grief.

Wolf of the world: he's at our door:
His rank snout worries every crack.
We've long since finished hoping for
Some sop or stroke to turn him back.

No fantasy survives his greed,
But proud of what he drives me to
I lift myself, your broken reed,
And I club at the wolf of the world for you.

After an Ancient Text

The *Elephant* is made, from hooves to thighs,
Unbendable, with legs that lack a knee.
If once he stretched out flat he'd never rise.
To sleep, he rests his bulk against a tree.

The hunter comes to know this sleeping habit,
And hacks the tree so nearly through that when
The *Elephant* returns to lean against it
Twelve brothers cannot lift him up again.

Oh helpless *Elephant!* The hunter hones
His knives, the beast is cooked, the flesh is gone—
Yet strength in the smoke of the burning bones,
A forest ghost, destroys serpent and demon.

Strutting Jackals

The lion can't preach to the jackal . . . ah
But he will, he will: "You scrounging cur,
Live large, enjoy, make time with the world
As it comes!" (for it comes, it always comes,
To lions). A jackal's yellow heart
Bears the pit of another fruit—unblessed
With the pulsing pyrotechnics
Of the lion, how he snickers, leers,
But ponders the kingly preachment, thinking
(And this accounts for the solitaires
And armies of strutting jackals) *yes,*
I must be more of a lion, if not
In fact, at least by reputation . . .
And takes up his awful fate.

Hometruths

Who sees her as she is sees she is
Beautiful, even bickering with
Her daughter, stirring the midnight soup
Discoursing, in one shoe.
                    We're all born
Hungry; few learn cookery
From that, and fewer still to risk
The courage of a style, that fierce
Intelligence.
                    She moves like the sound
Of bees; wanders nowhere far;
Goes at the speed of honey; is
Mellifluous, mellifluous,
Stronger than the lion
And his storms.

The Parent Birds

Two Junes we've watched their flights, stuffing
A young bird in the treehole here
By the long flat rocks of the old Finn quarries,
But can't decide between various claims
Out of Roger Tory Peterson: are they
Swifts? starlings?—we seem to go by
Their occupational appellation,
For mainly what they do is to light
On a short dead branch beside the nest hole—
Less a branch than a jutting twig—
Hop to the mouth of the hole and put
Grub or worm or whatever they've got
In. They rest in another locust
Till instinct stirs them off again.

My wife observes June's piety,
Rereading *Ulysses;* speaks of Joyce's
Conscious use of Mme. Blavatsky's
Doctrine called *Akasa:* nothing
Is ever lost on earth: a faith
In total conservation of being,
Each single word (almost wrote *bird*),
Each worm, grunt, breeze, typo,
Immortal. The wind runs very strong,
Cold and rain for six June days—
Every unlost gust keeps returning.
At times, platoons of Parent Birds,
Through interludes of less foul weather,
Peck the lawn for what the rain raises.

Today, inspecting the creaking tree—
The parent birds have been off duty—
As I watched, the yellow bill first,
Then streaky head, I saw the young bird
Gaze from its hole (later I joked
It looked dumb enough to fall. My daughter:
"Admit it: you think if you look away
One minute, that bird has had it!"). Okay,
I did feel it wore a worried air,
No feeding parents, the rainlashed wind,
An ominous creaking overhead . . .
I went back in, beneath my roof,
And it beneath its own . . . Leopold
Bloom tends, too, toward the maudlin

Regarding birds: shreds Banbury cakes
For the thankless, homeless gulls above
The Liffey, out in all weathers: makes
A verse upon them, later thinks
That is how poets write, the similar
Sounds, and *How can you own water really?*
It's always flowing in a stream.
Bored, my daughter says "The world's
Coming to an end," and then
"Why doesn't somebody write me a letter?"
We write each other letters, addressed
To opposite sides of the table where we
All three all day huddle
At our small electric fire.

Ill Will

O heavy-bellied Will I ride,
Slow tiger, better play it straight:
False sheepishness is out of date:
Your true stripes show beneath the wool
All unappeased and criminal—
Draw blood, crunch bone, be satisfied,
Ill Will!
      You gather strength and stealth
To fall at last . . . upon yourself.
Ah, foolish Will, to spin beneath
The skin to butter, tail in teeth.

Item

At daybreak on the beach, through mist,
Her horse immense, twice her size,
With a proper crop and hat and boots
A girl sedately rides; at once
Everything seems odd, the presence
Of everything; I think of the length
Of a horse's face, and his gentleness,
And his tilted teeth; of riders swerving
On horses; horses' urgency
Pulling, rearing . . . unrelentingly
Strange, this rage, this calm—it's said
That God began with light and salt,
But losing grip, perhaps, looks on
At the violence of being, boggled—
Armadillo: anteater: whale—
The whole unlikely drama swelling,
Veering toward an end, the action
Speeding till the long explosion's
Done . . . the first outrageous, helpless
Items disappear, the vision
Slowing through exclusion, running
Out, a fog of vacancy . . .
The unaccountable presence
Of a horse.

II

New Copley in the Gallery

"Portrait of Mrs. Ronald Cotton."
A plainness only a lover could love.

Show-offy lace at the wrists, gown
Copley might have painted before
On other women: had she worn it,
Deborah, née Mason? Perhaps already
Copied there in its green silk shimmer,
Out of a pattern book from London,
It waited to set her off, hair
Tight in a holiday ribbon, modest
Folded fan in her lap. Her placid
Gaze rebukes the unreal sheen
Of this dress, pinched-in waist, vision
Of womanly daintiness out of which
The Actual rises: thickening neck
Supporting a four-square visage: alderman's
Underchin, cheeks of a strong
Tun-maker, gentle eyes and a broadbrow
Nearly a match for a Pittsfield bear;
A female faith-of-Job, accepting
The given vessel of soul, body
Slimmed in the trappings of fantasy,
This over-large girl appears to concede
No hint of an absence of grace. None of us
Ever is good or pretty enough
To win the love we crave . . . each
A child in a grown-up's setting, pre-limned
Dress of a silver green, we stare,
Like this cherished wife of Ronald Cotton,
Bravely out at the viewer.

The Times

My daughter tells me her dream, where she saw
The Times on the porch in the morning and knew
From the page-sized black of the headlines— W A R —
D E C L A R E S   W A R—that now it was over, and wept
In her dream to think that she'd never have
Her years, friends, a marriage night,
Shifting the dreck of everyday life . . .
A young woman mourning, telling her father
Her dream, and he goes sadly in search
Of rage, he's able at anything
But rage: he will stretch out his arm, his hand,
Ashamed to see
How not a finger trembles.

Woman in the Subway

Once in the subway a downcast woman
Moved along the platform saying
"Talk to me? Talk to me?" No one replied.
Refusal—tight-lipped turning away—
Seemed the world's oldest profession, so when she
Reached me I spoke. "What?" I said,
And at once she lifted the word to her mouth
Like a frog from the swamp: "Ra-*whaaat?*" she mocked,
Turning in circles, blaring, as if
She'd won, she'd made someone speak, a fellow
Human: "Ra-*whaat?* Ra-*whaat?*"

The Pale Ones

A clearing: a burnt-out space: it was either
That, or they'd hack down altogether
The wilderness back of your eyes. So we scorched,
With the usual pain and help, the usual
Square for such a case—you built
Your hut with the wide veranda, achieved
The houseboy, all as it should be, the bottle
Of Jameson, volumes of Wharton and Maugham,
The white goat at the fence, the shrub
At the well. Now drain your glass, now fold
Your hands and nod to the sunset—nice.
Later the basic creatures will grunt
At the waterhole. But those that rushed
From the blaze at first, the shy amazing
Pale ones, appearing
Tottering, blinking
At your edges: have they gone
Beyond? back in? are they hiding? At times
When you think you sleep, near dawn, I listen,
And softly, very softly, I hear you
Call them.

Two Memory Poems

I

I still recall the poverty
Of students: meals of pasta, never
Tickets for ballet or Russian
Cigarettes. My smirk would fill
The mirror as I lightly held her,
Fright-gay girl I called back then
My woman. When she spoke my name
She changed my body—every time.
And now? Is she grand, is she silly now,
As I've become these twenty years
More grave? Does she sleep
With her glasses on?
Is she sad somewhere in curlers,
Eating fudge?

II

The light in the john,
As the wind blows strong,
Dims, suddenly sways, and the hallway's
Posters shake
In the path of the storm.
Nostalgia, that seeks perception very
Choosingly, as pod-silk floats
Toward ground, returns another day:
The streets were dark with rain: late,
Eighteen, in love, a bunch of jonquils
Bobbing in my hand, I ran
Street after gleaming street, not knowing
That she would wait; not knowing that she
Would wait.

Like This

In my box of a cinderblock office in Building
14, I doze on the narrow couch and you
Haven't phoned and it strikes me that lying
Dead will be packaged and cold and straight
Like this, exactly like this, only minus
The clock you bought me, the books, the sketch
Caren sent from Rome—and yes, of course,
No window, no rising to watch a boy
And his dog below; but otherwise just
Like death, only adding the chair the lamp the
Chess column clipped from the Thursday *Times* and your
Voice your laughter the wind on the way
To the car that claims it's real that says
It will slap my face awake or push me
Down or twist me in half if it wants to.

Working Title

Our working title is anger, lifting
The lids and throwing the new potatoes.
We voted once for the final solution
Of silence, massive withholding, death
& taxes. Now our stop-signed street
Is a crazy flashing green at a cat's-cradle
Scatterramp intersection, you shouting
Left, me right, both wrong and cracking
Up, what matter,
We'd go with each other
Any way at all.

Laundry Day

The static from your leotard
Is indefensible (it's Laundry Day)—O,
Deep farm-fetish
Of a city boy,
You're ripe beyond
Redress!
        We play
Our wants by ear, by whim and risk,
Because it's hateful what the Whitecoats say,
The needle-eyed Behaviorists:
That we're mere gene-tools, robots, biomanic itch—
So likewise hens and cocks achieve a use,
That thinskinned eggs might reproduce—
Mere moving parts
To please some cunning chromosome,
And nevermind our mounting wildly up
On dialogue, or feeling sadly stirred
By news reports of bedmates whose disease,
The Screaming Me-Me's,
Changed sex
To a one-letter
Word.
        Look,
Gene Queen, maybe I'm
In fact your fully automated
King Kong, pure
Extremity . . .
But how you knock me
Out, see here it's
Laundry Day:

The Eyes of Bendix
Are upon me, Maytag's
Lifting off new payloads bound
For Mars!
                    So moist, this atmosphere;
Each robot takes a folding chair
While dryers hum and clean-freaks thumb
McCall's.
                    There's little more to do
Than contemplate how my brave blue
Undershorts go plunging past
Again, like true
Meridian . . .
And now your flighty petticoat
Sinks down—our sheets won't sun in coun-
Try air, but oh we may be getting
There—unfree of will, okay, but
Name a better way to serve
Our time.
                    The busy genes can just
Ignore us, at their consoles brooding
Management design . . . or will they
Gaze up from their print-outs, cheer
Like monitors at Houston as we
Dock and phase
Our breathing, over-
Reaching worldly
Thought?
                    We'll turn
This fresh sheet down, and then lift up

The warm nightgown . . . to genes we're vast we're
Very far
Away . . . hello, it's
Laundry Day . . .

III

Hand of the Mind

Now pause a while, the rest of your life kept waiting,
As an older woman dries her hands on her apron,
Finds for the camera's sake a pleasant smile.
Let me hold you here in my mind, a gift of sadness,
For already you move away down the flood of years,
As I touch your hair, as I rest my hand on your shoulder;
As the hand of my mind moves lightly now upon you.

Finding a Yiddish Paper on the Riverside Line

Again I hold these holy letters,
Never learned. Dark candelabras.

Once they glowed in the yellow light
Through the chicken smell of Friday night,

My father in his peach-stained shirt
Scrubbing off twelve hours' dirt

While I drew my name on misted glass.
Now trim suburban houses pass

And on my lap the headlines loom
Like strangers in the living room.

Across the Hall

I hear you naming names, students,
Iris Dellums, Lois Ann
McCann: shadowy smiling faces
Slide in a yearbook progress back
Of my eyes. Reading names, setting
Grades perhaps, preparing a list
By dictation, calling roll: *Mary*
Rietz, Mimsi Bressler, Arbor
Helms. Saying them out, saying them
Each one out in your poet's level
Manner, each with an edge, a border
Of pause, matte of dignity made
By your rhythm, tongue, bronze and watery
Blade of words. Even as
You speak I'm mourning you, and me,
And *Muffy Brown.* Slow-moving passage.
Every week and year everywhere
Officers preachers dictators foremen
Name them name them *Anna Teplock*
Marnie Zimmer Barbara Pachman
Bless the living bless the living
Celia Benjamin
Irma Jean O'Neil

Complain

She listens to my case, is mild
And fair, and still I complain, complaint's
My *metier*, my breath, my very
Metronome. What I really need
Is an enemy. Should I advertise?
For someone to stand in the way, to cast
A darkness so deep that not even crabgrass
Would grow . . .?—a beast who'd glue unspeakable
Lies about me on walls? I could bathe
In his bile, he would workmanlike spit in my soup
Bowl after bowl all my days, my humpbacked
Shadow blown up large who'd say
"Complain? I'll give you reason to complain!"

The Beautiful Suicide

Sometimes she wanted so much to burn
She drew up everybody's air.

We had to leave her then, leave
Or die.

Now, she's not
Anywhere.

She breathed at once
The whole of the dark,

Plenty of that
For us all.

We Others

A bunch of slumming college professors,
Six of us, boozing, bluffing at nickel-
Ante, and she comes in, goes round
Shaking every hand . . . now why should I
Simply assume that something disgusting,
Air of sweat and stables, cigars,
Alerts her fine disdain, that she'd need
To get out, and quick, clearly not
Her scene? I suppose I believe she could hardly
Expect to be one of the boys. I think:

> they live in a weather of waiting, always
> lonely, somehow, endlessly bearing
> gifts to a raucous Presence who may
> despise them. *Come after, come after,* say
> their fragrant glances: *follow this randy*
> *sweetness; this humid*
> *trail.*

Not one of us
Likely to grab for her butt, or even
Cause a laugh as she leaves (as she does)
By playing Groucho's Priapian part,
Eye-rolling quips about full-bodied women;

And yet, as if by a pool in the mist,
While all of us reek with the oiled steel
Of the hunt, I see her stand and distantly,
Dreamily hear us pass, we others

Who clatter along our crazy way
With our dogs and our horns and our horses.

30

Stuff

What's right about all this clutter, say
The carrying straps looping down from the rings
Of the cameras, four in a row on their backs
On the blue-painted shelf by the window, lenses
Up like cups for rain, or the broom

And ironing-board in the corner, the Smith
Corona with last week's 'always-stop-
At-the-top-of-a-page' still in there, reading
"Away and think of something," awaiting
Thought, is the thought of the suchness hands

Arrange: it's you who've left this cup
Just here, just here, we're real, our stuff
Comes falling into line against
Inflation, depression, the succulents
In their little white plastic pots, the prints,

All messages received, or life's mere
Miles, mere heavy miles for the man
In the jouncing Memphis coach who shouts
"Fresh horses! Maps! A side of beef!
Say, can't you speed it up?—I'm in a hurry!"

Malediction

You who dump the beer cans in the lake;
Who in the strict woods sow
The bulbous polyethylene retorts;
Who from your farting car
With spiffy rear-suspension toss
Your tissues, mustard-streaked, upon
The generating moss; who drop
The squamules of your reckless play,
Grease-wrappers, unspare parts, lie-labeled
Cultures even flies would scorn
To spawn on—total Zed, my kinsman
Ass-on-wheels, my blare-bred bray
And burden,
                may the nice crabs thread
Your private wilds with turnpikes; weasels'
Condoms squish between your toes,
And plastic-coated toads squat *plop*
Upon your morning egg—may gars
Come nudge you from your inner-tube,
Perch hiss you to the bottom, junked,
A discard, your dense self your last
Enormity.

Old Men at the Edge of the Highway

What they think about,
What they think about,
Is that something's happening faster without
Their permission, within and without, and will simply
Continue, whatever they think to say
Or do, will simply continue, and that's
What they think about,
What they think about,
Walking along the highway
Against the traffic.

Local Messages

Legs

We put out we put out but never for long
Even surpass each other we're humble we
Hope wherever this passenger goes
There'll be dancing.

Penis

I monument the city state,
Guardian of treasure—you
Can't make me point and fetch but rather
Treat with me by embassies—
Through deference we yet may turn out
Friends, we have enough in common:
Noble and Idiot both, Prince
And Frog.

Stomach

Which of us plays the mother? First
I'm wishes; then you flee to me
As to home. Each of us croons, rocking:
"Rest, my child, my child."

Hands

About us no confusions, we're
Your scatterboxes, mean to carry

On—not even thought can hope
To stop us.

Hair

You love us best! Confess! We get
Rapt care . . . oh, if we made a sound
We'd giggle! If they shot you out
From under, still we'd grow—as we
Are cherished, we'll be saved—father!
Patriot of our nation!

Untitled

Your labels or your life! Strip off
These labels, bulldoze your billboards, nothing
Behind them but your wants, your friends
Are standing in the doorway
To the backroom, grinning, grinning, how to
Choose? well, choose them all: don't be
The woman in the curlers any
Longer, nor the one who smirks
About her: slide
Down the whitewater rapids—
Belly along the rapids, whoever
You are.

IV

Glee

Right for a bounce on our sagging bed
We buried the phone by its ear in the pillow
But came a buzz like the voice of cancer,
ABUSER! WE'RE BLASTING THROUGH! CONNECTIONS
REMAIN UNMET! YOU'RE OFF THE HOOK, YOU'RE
Making love by the numbers, like science . . .
Somehow   you're counting   the strokes.

Keaton's College *(1927)*

Timid, bookloving Momma's boy
In a shrinking suit, pure Fauntleroy,
Buster's off to College, to win
His lady with a Letter . . . but lacks
All grace: a soda jerk, his eggs
Miss his shakes, and when he covers third
The balls bound by, they give him the raspberry,
Dirge on the snare and kazoo—but Clarissa's
Locked in her room with the villain, oh no!
—Now our hero brokenfield *runs*, he broadjumps,
Vaults through the window, discus-throws
And bats the cad, a one-man stand
Of sportliness, Merriwell
Himself! "You know what this means?" asks the Dean,
Finding them clinched. She says, "Oh yes!
It means we're getting married!" What yens
For virtue and romance! They enter
The chapel (one-second shot) they emerge
In a cloud of rice (one second) right off
(Two seconds) angry and middleaged
They're snapping at the children now they're
Doddering, wait, hold on, two gravestones
Side-by-side THE END what's this?—
For a six-second sequence he worked through his bookish
Weakness, conquered the playingfields:
Marriage, kids, the grave?—is that why
He took off like Jesse Owens? and she,
For this she gave up
Her college degree?

Her Atmosphere

1

At first it's cool, her atmosphere;
But after a time you find her there,
Like edelweiss on the mountain.

2

She dives into change, deep pendulum—
Or fights it out along one line
If it takes the whole damn summer.

3

She marks the depth, a stake in the tide—
The high, the low . . . let them trip on her,
She stands.

4

She turns her eyes to the world and I see
Whatever she sees, like invisible ink
Over flame.

On the One Known Daguerreotype
of Emily Dickinson

Doer of cunning packets, soul's
Sachet, heart-salt poetry—
Dry-wine Muse with tight-back parted
Hair, eyes that tease their creaturely
Sadness, thoughtless mouth too rich
In yearning yet for irony,
For wrenching hymns, the whole occult
Affair, she's here like anyone
Eighteen, flower in hand, elegant
Gown: daring publicity,
A reader by Amherst's electric light,
Sister, daughter, belle, baker
Of pies (nine, one manic day!)
—For once to risk full openness,
So wanting love to see!

Counting the Losses
For Helen Corsa

Yeats, who mourned youth's sweetness gone
  All that is lost is the body
Slept, he said, on boards, to turn
His verses hard, and hardened sung
Solace for the ox-eyed, stunned
Animal of desire. Rossini,
Shocked by his mother's death, gave over
Music with its grandeur, became
A chef—a sort of mother—seeking
To yield the milk of consolation.
Goya, beauty's nightmare lover,
Mad from leadwhite, vicious war,
Saw his Duchess, named for dawn,
In the form of a toad, in the yellow gloom
Of a circus, sickly, running down;
He painted children with massive heads,
A giant bestriding a hillside; etched
A chicken plucked alive by fiends
  All that is lost is the body.

Approaching composition the laureate
  All that is lost is the body
Said and resaid his name like the clack
Of British Railways: *Tennyson,*
Tennyson-Tennyson, murmuring
Of innumerable *be's*—mere being,
Humiliating history.
Heinrich Schliemann, final hero
Of Troy, saw as a child a tombstone:
"Here lies Heinrich Schliemann"—(a brother,

Dead in infancy)—"Beloved
Son" *himself! in the grave!* He told
Lies to the Turks, would have killed to continue
Digging for Helen's balconies,
For Priam's gate; a lifetime, raising
The other from the dead. That all
We suffer be raised and opened, that
Is our portion, work, to lift from the grave—
He who digs is the living son

All that is lost is the body.

Spacks Street

Fame: fame: whole generations
Going up in pique, uncalled,
Unchosen! Silly to waste much strength
Earning a place of note (there's not
A grave without
Its certified *has-been*)—
But once . . . I wanted a star in my name;
Or a state, a river, a unit of measure . . .
A street, at least . . . Spacks Street . . . Spacks Place . . .
How nice! Imagine the little kids
Playing Giant Steps after dinner in summer,
Leaping from one of your curbs to the other.
Or someone moves, does well, gains weight
And years and accolades, and says
"God, if they only could see me today,
The old gang
Back on Spacks Street!"

Old-Time Stereopticon

Depth of life once you bring it together till   both sides spring into focus—at first it's
    tricky, teasingly   two: twin alps or
        bike   bike
        farm woman   farm woman

—instructions tell you to blink, twiddle   the knobs, stare at an object ("avoiding
the faces") until the subject the subject   explodes into every dimension—the whole
dear multitude! But sometimes scene   after each scene keeps double, flat, refuses
    the richer sense. Affection is also   known to balk like that. Some claim

at once they find a way, each view   rising instantly full, but as for
    me, I have to   twiddle, blink
        each time   each time
        avoiding   the faces.

The Need to Praise

The stained-glass flair
Of a bluejay's rear
Or the stunning size
Of Cincinnati,
Of all the needs
The need to praise
—Winter, even;
Even rough weather—
Fats the jagged cord of truth
And lifts the heart from its soggy floor
Till you're liable to gather fondness for
The greasebright river: whatever: whatever:
Rainy mornings!
Mothers-in-law!

Rehearsal

Hardly dawn . . . yet just beyond
My window this mockingbird
Starts his day, he
Works at phoebe, peewee, jay,
Extending his repertoire.
                              I imagine
He's at it early, with few awake
To criticize, since part of his act
Seems wobbly, being new.
                              For a change,
As a self-conscious kid at an upright will shift
From next week's killing piece to the speed
Of conquered, steady scales, he'll do
Some down-pat flawless calls, impressions
Of mourning dove? American eagle?
—Things he's been using for years . . . then back
To a stab at basso crow, feeling
His way, rehearsing, true professional . . .

Those he imitates may rise
Late—they wake
To a simpler calling,
Filling the air with their constant, unchanging,
Owned and original cries.

Seeing Pablo Neruda

One fall day I saw Pablo Neruda,
Small as life, crossing Plimpton Street,
Unnoted, wearing a hard expression.
His thought's on the bombing, I thought, endless
Bombing—and even I might possibly
Not have known it was Pablo Neruda,
Except just an instant before I'd seen,
In the Grolier Bookstore, his photo, pausing
To maybe buy the Belitt and Reid
Translations. A latin lady held
His arm, or rather his elbow, the way you
Do with a Maestro—be careful, Maestro,
The traffic!—I *think* it was
Pablo Neruda,
Passing part of his residence
On earth, perhaps in town to visit
His fellow diplomat-poet Octavio
Paz, could be, who knows, such things
Aren't sure, but what struck me was I wanted
To follow, I wanted to shout *Hey, somebody,*
Look, look, that's Pablo Neruda!
The Chilean poet! Ambassador
To France!

*

I was talking to Mary Kaye, who sells
Her pottery masks on a sliding scale
As a spit-in-the-eye
To the price-tagging world,

So you give what you can if you want one of Mary's
Works, say the bas-relief
Of a sun god.

*

The Product—that's what it's all about—
I see a girl gussied up in a sheep-fleece
Coat, and that's the Product . . . I hear
A praiser in the hall, a student
Listens, a stock
Goes up,
And that's
The Product.

*

Pablo Neruda, Nobel Prize,
Made a speech in New York, said the South American
Future was finally on, there he goes,
Past Leavitt & Pierce's, The Holyoke Center,
And no one but me
To *recognize!*

*

(And what if it *wasn't*
Pablo Neruda?)

*

50

(What if it was
Octavio Paz?)

*

The Product, it's there on the Big Board, it's death
To de-fuse, it's you in your *soi-disant* Chilean
Sheep rancher's raunchy coat, valued person, your
Super-low sexy voice, your glances
Around sheep's collars, now
Who wouldn't buy?

*

Pray, if you ever see Pablo Neruda—
Who praised his socks, who damned the whores
And the profits, the sickly horror of profit
And loss—pray to be Not For Sale;
To walk the earth in the pride of life;
To give as much as you can.

The Ventnor Waterworks

I was holding the phone, desperate, you know,
—The burnt-out coil, the warranty refund—
Waiting to scream at the claims adjuster

When out of the past a chill green pleasure
Rose through my body: summers riding
My bike to the Ventnor Waterworks
To drink from the cold of its fountain. I'd enter

As if at a temple: no human sound:
Ferns, everywhere ferns and a passionate
Coolness—and here I am, thirty years later,

Shouting like any maniac,
Steward of sour grapes, "I want
My car! That's not my problem, I want
My car!"

Elegy

Mother, you used to sit there, staring,
As year followed year at the nursing home;
Nothing but sleep on your mind by the end.

You'd try to hide your teeth in the drawer,
Wanting that comfort, but we, we'd tell you
To open up, slipping them in
—As if you weren't a child again.

Together we used to dump the sacks
Of Maine potatoes: how heavy they were!
Sift of dirt; stumble of flesh.

We bricked the dates and stacked the oranges—
Tucked the tissues to steady the pears
In their boxes. Remember Mr. Plum,
Mother? Remember Mr. Gosling?

Lintonia's Greek-style turkey wing
With coffee for lunch, 95 cents . . . ?
Then back we'd go, to ring 'em up,

Mother, in our white jackets:
The mushrooms, the cherries, the lettuces;
The ease to the mouth of freestone peaches;
The just-washed spinach, cool to the hand.

Like a Prism

On any particular morning
The paunchy gent in the basement room,
Not feeling like Sancho or Falstaff, is laughed at
By boys who see him, half awake,
Through the grating, and know they'll never, ever,
Look like that, bloated, sad,
Pleased by nothing
But sleep . . . on a normal
Morning in this world, while the new bride
Slips away, excited, to count
Her sheets still pampered in tissues, and many
Die of the drought, or their color, or taste
In justice, there's something
We want will not
Be given, we blessed
Of the day—a bitter
Dream curves down our mouths to a state
Of iron—we need the password, exemption
From guilt and grief, for we are no longer
Struck to learn that the torturer works
His wonders on any
Particular morning.

We need for God himself to say
All right, all right to be fed, to take up
Space on the planet, to
Cherish the day, to
Draw a share, like a prism,
Of its light.

V

In Arnold's Orchard

Yearning to pluck from a roped-off tree
In Arnold's Apple Orchard, it struck me
That even before the greed of sin,
No one but Eve to stir my yen,
I'd have felt deprived. One life. One woman.
Of course, I only speak of what's common,
Counting myself, like any old Adam,
A happily married man.

The Two of Them

Sometimes the two of them get in the kitchen,
Cook up a storm for hours, dicing
The onions, fast-fingered, keeping ahead
Of the tears . . . or something greener, the fall's last
Pesto—pausing for platefuls of flatcut
Tomatoes with pepper and basil they're making it
Happen: deep dish blueberry pie:
No need for books of lore, though they have them,
Copper bowl, chilled whisk, they'll settle
For Woolworth ovenwear, one big spoon,
Saying "Mmmm,mmmm, just taste!"—they'll settle
For that.

Imagining a Unicorn

After the Unicorn Tapestries at The Cloisters

"Theoretically, there exists a perfect possibility of happiness: to believe in the indestructible element in oneself and not strive after it."—Kafka, *Parables and Paradoxes*

I

With greyhounds and with running hounds
You gather to hunt the unicorn,
Grave seignors in the flowery field—
Spirit that leaps with earthweight on,
Noble spirit, white as the wind—
You seek his trail with spears in hand,
"That furious beast, His precious horne"
Turning to dove-song every poison,
Asp of envy, kiss of assassin.
"The greatness of his mynde is such
He chooseth rather to dye than be taken."

*

White, whole-of-the-spectrum white,
Come from afar, like starlight,
He kneels beside the sullied waters,
Drawing the venom into himself
While lion and leopard, stinking hyena,
Wait to drink. He dips his horn,
Noblesse oblige; untouchably bright.
The peacock meets his face in the fountain.
The hunters wait until he leaps:
Law of the chase. That others may drink:
Charity, in an animal dream!

*

He rushes on, quarry of kings:
By walnut, linden, trembling aspen,
Periwinkle, "joy of the ground,"
Forget-me-nots of Mary's color.
Takes to the stream; defends himself.
A dog's impaled, aie! aie!
Water-, wind-, fireheart-white:
By hawkweed, bluebell, primrose, clary,
Speared, surrounded—untamable—
And yet he enters the rose-wound fence,
The virgin's thorn-crowned loveliness.

II

For passion we seek you, goat-chinned horse,
Lover and teacher, feral Christ:
Holy body that never lies;
Among us as long as we think you are—
By orange tree, madonna lily,
Always the maiden's one intended,
Cragpacer, dog-killer, furious source
For those who wove your tapestry,
Spinning your rosebuds out of the worm,
And thistles saying 'Mary,' 'Mary'—
Rapt-eyed image of charity.

*

Among the partridges, plump as lust,
Christ, little buket, whatever your name,

Held by a woman's gentle touch,
Now you are ready to take your death,
Spirit that draws its earthweight on;
More than us yet close to us,
Soul that enters its earthly home
Amid the oak, the beech, the palm,
Pattern of beauty's brilliance, strangeness;
Beauty of violence; beauty of calm;
This flood: this sleep: these marriages.

*

Noblesse oblige: ready for death
As her handmaiden waves the spearsmen in.
Called to his death, mysterious,
By the horn of the hunter Gabriel.
Bowing down, bowing down, fully strong,
To the salted wounds of sacrifice:
Spear in the neck, spear in the side
—Only we would seek to destroy him,
We in our terror of worthlessness—
Dogs on his back: substantial God;
Torn by the world; rose-touched; dead.

III

They bear the corpse to the royal city,
And there a little boy turns away,
Petting his dog: will not look, for sorrow.

61

And there a lady turns away,
Seeing the bridegroom wreathed with thorn,
On trodden flowers, heavily borne.
Nightingale in the medlar bush,
Squirrel in the hawthorne boughs obscured,
Little city with bannerettes,
Coopers and cooks, saddlers and gossips—
This sadness, over and over again.

*

Are you still in our world, great unicorn?
You who drew the rage of men
Into you like a poison—returned,
Always renewed, a gift to us,
—Plenitude upon plenitude—
Curing our wants with fruits and flowers,
Who kill as a charm for deathlessness.
You who have bled, your wounds are gone,
The blood you shed from the vicious hunt
Juice of love-apple, staining your coat,
O holy body that never lies!

*

Hunters, your greed would drink his strength—
See, he returns; his wounds are gone.
Princely, forgiving, unendingly born,
He marries the garden of the earth,
Plenitude upon plenitude,

The cuckoopint and paquerette;
Butterfly, bittern, gnat, civet—
Frog and bee and startled rabbit—
Plenitude, plenitude!—wild strawberry;
Duck and dog and feverfew;
Daisy—day's eye—sun as a flower;

The hazeltree, and the holly.

Don Potts and His Visionary Cars

Potts. Potts. Think of the name:
Plod-along, pottering *Potts* . . . no wonder
He built these dreamer's chassis, pleasured by
Silkspun bearings, double-sleeked manifolds,
Polishments of speed: no pistons
Slapping, spatter of fire and sludge,
But a pure, a boyish power, ceaseless
Purr to the eye and the bodysense,
Hephaestus with his limp becoming
A prettier god, Apollo, Apollo,
Who used to go *pocketa-pocketa*, had to go
Potts-potts-potts.

Gliding

In Memory of Timothy Holm, 1954-1973

You put your faith in calamity—
Flying, falling, your constant themes.
"Winds rage," you wrote,
"In my hollow body."

You told in class of an August day
Crossing the Mass. Ave. Bridge, seeing
A jumper—you dived after, too late
To reach him where he forced himself under.

In traffic once in Central Square
I gave you the horn and the arm and you grandly
Slowed. Ignoring the honking drivers,
You bike-turned laid-back circles around me.

If only we'd see you
Gliding through sunrise
With all the time in the world, a never-
Sullied will . . . someone to pray to.

High on the currents of air you dived,
Dawn on the opposite cliffside glowing
Clay-red. *"Either
A gust or a lull."*

Wise-guy, impatient
Of fat-assed comfort,
You courted jokes: *"Ten percent of all
Giraffe babies / die from the fall."*

You passed the brink, spread against wings,
Harnessed to speed, yielding, borne,
Till a trick of wind slammed you down too hard.
Who could raise you, pick up the pieces?

We, with no spirit to pray to, mourn
Your body's strength, worshipping risk:
Your zest, now each fine wind contains
Your ghost. You were a brightness, passing

Among us, Tim.
You dreamed you could fly.
*"Like dandelions
We are blown away."*

A Normal Noon

I was standing in line to pay the cashier
For my swiss and tomato sandwich, my carton
Of fat-free milk, when the lunchroom lights
Went off; flashed on and off. A woman
Reached for her bag of laundry; three
Math hacks looked up, amazed, from their figures . . .
We all know the signal's the radio,
A siren, not blinking lights, but see
How we live now, see how anything odd
Can almost make us suspect that we're having
Our final scene, with the afternoon's work
On a memo at the office. Stopped
Pocketing change! With a stupid mouthful
Of beans! Of course, the lights held firm;
Simply a meaningless power failure;
A normal noon, nothing
About to happen.

The Man with Orange Wands

Returned, and weary-spirited,
I find again I'm gazing down
At this man with orange wands in his high
Lordship: at my same hometown
Man at the end of the runway, firm
In self-importance as a tree,
Too much in charge for speech (*good plane,
Slow, slow*, he waves; *play dead*)—a man
Who's never had to move to reach
The center of the world.

People

Some choose themselves for the guarantee—
Return unopened, your money back.

Some try every chocolate in the box—
Must be a nougat somewhere!

Some daren't kiss: frogs are pompous enough—
Who wants to cope with Princes?

Some swing, like mental/genital
Dutch doors.

Many seem brave: "*What* clothes?" they say.
Others, more rare: "What Emperor?"

Several, cogs, plan to invent
The wheel.

A few will greet each summer's return
Like a kindness from a stranger.

Once one said to me, "You are
The river of my life."

Gerard

For Nicole Pinsky

The easels went to the swift, namely
Irving Berman and me, back
When I was in kindergarten, Nicole.
Two easels, so we raced, come arts
& crafts. I usually won, am strange
About winning yet: sometimes even
Hang back a bit who early shoved
My way, intense to make it, first
To get there first, and only then
To love the giant bottles of yellow
And blue and schloshing around on the paper
Various genius items, and all
This while Gerard would sit in his corner:
He always accepted the banging-sticks
In the orchestra, the rest of us calling
"Me! Me!" for the glockenspiel;
Gerard the heavily-mothered, lost
The first day, tearful, beating the door,
His mother gone and couldn't hear him
No matter how hard he cried, as teacher
Explained, and next day the same, what luscious
Sport, Gerard with his oval head
And museum guard demeanor, convenient
Gerard—forced to wear rubbers, galoshes,
Black floppers every day, and every
Day a man's black umbrella, imagine,
Even in breathless June, grim
Mr. Junior Death Gerard with shame
On his feet, above his head, we almost
Died, Lenny and Irving and Wilma

70

And Neil and Shirley and Marvin and me:
Wizened Gerard, saved from the rain—
Gerard, Gerard, we called your name
Till you wept: that hushed us a bit, and then:
>Gerard, Gerard,
>Momma's pet!
>Gerard, Gerard,
>Don't get wet!

(Am I telling you this for forgiveness, Nicole?
I hear at your kindergarten you flinch
At the sudden shrill of the schoolyard bell;
Can't bear the noise and confusion; it's good
Your teacher lets you in before
The rest, but please, if they start to shout
>Nicole, Nicole,
>Jump in a hole!

Or other stuff like that, will you kindly
Let us know, and we'll fix it up
Somehow, we lords of creation?)—meanwhile
Gerard's a judge by now I'd guess,
Or a millionaire, or both, with regular
Habits—or what if he turned out folksy,
Just Plain Bill, why not? or a hairy
Prophet, a poet, a singing waiter,
Anything, engineer or enter-
Tainer, amazement to wife and kids
And friends, no permanent damage—but oh
Come back Gerard, and we'll take off your rubbers,
We'll fracture that damned umbrella in 12,000
Pieces, we'll lock your mother in

The room with the little chairs, we'll lift you
Shoulder high, home to our ethnic
Slovenly moms and pops who'll feed you
Kasha with bowties, *flanken* and gravy,
And let you stay up, *on a school night*, for Mr.
Keen, Gang Busters, Norman Corwin
Presents, and pack you off next day
Happy, straight through the pouring rain.